Walking In The Miraculous

Walking In The Miraculous

A 30 Day Devotional

Chad Gonzales

Walking In The Miraculous – A 30 Day Devotional
ISBN 13: 978-0-9777380-4-5
Copyright © 2009 by Chad Gonzales
www.ChadGonzales.com
All rights reserved. Printed in the USA

Cover design by: David Porter

Preface

Philippians 2:5 NIV
Your attitude should be the same as that of Christ Jesus.

If I am to have the same attitude, if I am to have the same thoughts and mindset as Jesus, I need to know what gave Him the attitude and confidence to do all He did on the earth.

The answer? Jesus realized His union with God. Day after day, through His study of the Law and His time spent fellowshipping with God, Jesus discovered who He was: He was one with God. Thus, Jesus began to learn about the ability of God that He possessed and the call of God upon His life.

In the same respect, as a believer, we have been made one with Christ. It is in our unity with Christ that we find how we should think, how we should feel and how we should view ourselves.

Jesus Christ is the standard for every believer; yet, in order for us to raise ourselves to the Standard, we must begin to think like Him and see ourselves in Him.

This devotional is meant to help you see your unity in Christ, your ability in Christ and all He has made you to be! Take each day and let it be your meditation all day long. Grab hold of the realities of who you are in Christ and begin living the life God designed for every believer: a life lived in the miraculous!

Day 1

ALL AUTHORITY

Matthew 28:18 NIV
Then Jesus came to them and said, "All authority in heaven and on earth has been given to me."

Look at the ministry of Jesus on the earth and see all the miracles that He performed. Then, consider His statement in John 14:12 that those who believe in Him would do the same works that He did and even greater works. Some Christians have dared to believe it, but even then, we've allowed an unrighteous mindset to stick with us. We still think we need more power, more authority, more this and more that to get the job done. Well, let me help you out with this nonsense.

When Jesus sent the 12 disciples out to heal the sick, Jesus said, "I give you authority over sickness and disease. Heal the sick, cleanse the lepers and raise the dead." Afterwards, when the ministry became larger, Jesus sent out 70 more disciples and said the same thing.

In John 17:5, when Jesus was praying to the Father in the Garden of Gethsemane, He said, "Now Father, restore unto me the glory and honor I had before I came to the Earth." In other words, Jesus wasn't walking in everything He had in Heaven. (You can also see this in Philippians 2:7).

So when we couple together all of Jesus' statements, we see something extraordinary: during Jesus earthly ministry, He wasn't walking in all authority Heaven had to offer. Only after His death, burial and resurrection was Jesus given all authority and all power in Heaven and in Earth.

So what does that mean for me and you? It means we can do the works of Jesus and even greater works because we are operating in more authority than Jesus was when He was on the Earth. I know that's a tremendously bold thing to say, but it's true; Jesus reveals His increase in authority in Matthew 28!

Jesus didn't send out the disciples with all authority and power until after His resurrection. Why? He didn't have it; but thank God, now He does! And because He does, we do too! After His defeat of Satan, Jesus gave us what He obtained. We are one with Christ! As He is, so are we in this world!

You don't need more authority, more power, more anointing, more gifts, etc. Stop waiting for more; you have all authority to get the job done! You can do it just like Jesus and have the very same results.

Confession:
I have authority over Satan and all of his friends. I have authority over all sickness and all disease. I don't need more because I have more than enough; I have an ample supply to get the job done! I can expect to have the same results as Jesus!

Day 2

YOUR ABILITY IN CHRIST

Ephesians 2:10 MSG
He creates each of us by Christ Jesus to join him in the work
he does, the good work he has gotten ready for us to do, work
we had better be doing.

Too many times, we doubt whether we can do what God has
called us to do. Too many times, we question whether we can fulfill
God's plan for our lives; we wonder if we have what it takes and
ponder our ability to get the job done.

When we stepped into Christ, we stepped out of our inability. We
stepped out of inferiority and we stepped into all things are possible!
Notice our text: God created us in Christ so we could join Him in
the work He has for us. For you to question your ability as a man in
Christ is to question the very ability of God.

God doesn't call the qualified; He qualifies the called. He called
you to His work in your mother's womb. When you accepted Christ
as your Lord and Savior, when you became one with Christ, God
qualified you.

So when you read the Word and you see an area that God wants
you to tweak in your life, remember that God has given you the

ability to do it.

When you begin to think about God's calling for your life, remember that God has given you the ability to fulfill it.

God has work for us and we better be doing it because He has enabled us to do so. When you stepped into Christ, the excuses went away!

<u>Confession:</u>
In Christ, I have the ability of God to get the job done. I can do everything He said in His Word because He has qualified me. I can be everything He has called me to be. I can fulfill all that He has called me to do.

Day 3

YOU'VE GOT THE GOODS

Colossians 2:10 NLT
So you also are complete through your union with Christ, who is the head over every ruler and authority.

Why is it that we are still struggling to get what God has said is already ours? We cry out for more peace. We cry out for more love. We cry out for more power and we even sing it in our songs. A very common song sung in churches all over the world has the following verse: "more love, more power, more of You in my life." Yet, Romans 5 says the love of God has been poured out into our hearts. How did it get there? When we became one with Christ!

Kenneth E. Hagin once told the story of a meeting he had with some fellow pastors. They were all talking about how they all needed to get more love. After some time of Kenneth Hagin just sitting there and not saying anything, the pastors finally asked his opinion on the matter. Kenneth E. Hagin responded, "If you need more love, you need to get saved!"

How much more love can you get? We have the peace of God, the faith of God, the joy of God, the love of God and the list goes on and on. You have the ability of Jesus, the anointing of the Holy Ghost, and the name of Jesus at your disposal. You are righteous through and through, blood bought, and blood covered. You have the grace of God and the self-control of God to say "No" to any sin or addiction that tries to come against you. You have the faith of God to move mountains and bring down any stronghold.

Don't let the devil whisper in your ear, "You don't have enough to get the job done." Rebuke that! You are complete in Christ. Christ isn't incomplete; He isn't lacking anything and if you are in Him, then you aren't either.

You have all the goods to get the job done. Anything that limits you in fulfilling and completing all God has called you to do and be...is bottled in religion and from the pit of hell! Stop working to get more of what God has already filled you to overflowing with!

Confession:
I am complete in Christ. I am missing nothing, lacking nothing. I am whole in Him. I have all the goods, all the abilities, and all the talents I need to fulfill God's call on my life. God is in me. If I am in union with Christ, there is no possible way for me to be lacking anything.

Day 4

ONE WITH GOD

John 10:29-30 NKJV
29 My Father, who has given them to Me, is greater than all; and no one is able to snatch them out of My Father's hand. 30 I and My Father are one.

This statement is one of the major keys to the miraculous life of Jesus. Jesus did not perform miracles because He was God; Jesus performed these miracles because He was a Man anointed by God allowing God to work through Him. Jesus did the miraculous as the Son of Man; Jesus did the miraculous as the Second Adam.

Philippians 2 shows us the mindset that Jesus had: "Jesus thought it not robbery to be equal with God." That was His mindset in Heaven and that was His mindset on earth. This understanding was the backbone of Jesus' ministry - His union with God.

All throughout His earthly ministry, Jesus speaks about His oneness with God. This understanding is what propelled Him into the miraculous and gave Him the confidence to do all that He did. Remember, all the miracles Jesus did on the earth, He did as a Man anointed by God.

Acts 10:38 says, "How God anointed Jesus Christ of Nazareth." In other words, it would be the same as saying, "How God anointed

Chad of Texas." Jesus operated as a man and stated that as a man, He was one with God.

You and I are no different than Jesus in this aspect. We are children of God, anointed by God and because of our union with Christ, we are also one with God. This is why miracles are normal for us. This is one of the major truths Satan does not want you to understand - because when you do, you will begin to replicate the ministry of Jesus on the earth with perfection.

Confession:
I am one with God. Because of my union with God, I can operate on this earth exactly as He would. My union with God puts me in a position to work signs, wonders and miracles. Miracles are normal for me!

Day 5

OF GOD

1 John 4:4 NKJV
You are of God, little children, and have overcome them, because He who is in you is greater than he who is in the world.

Let's key in on two important words within this passage of scripture: *of God.* Do you realize how powerful these two words are? One definition of the word *of* is "to indicate origin or derivation." In other words, your origin is from God; you were derived from God. Everything He is, it is in you. God's character, His faithfulness, peace, love and joy; all that He possesses is in you.

Remember when God made Adam? Look back in Genesis and see what He said. God said, "Let us make man in our image and likeness." When He made man, it was like looking into the mirror. That's why you are so good looking - you look just like the Creator!

God put Himself into you and I. When we accepted Jesus as Lord and Savior, we became a new creature, a new creation. We became born of God and fully flooded with Him. His wisdom was imparted to us, His faith was imparted to us, His power and authority was imparted to us, His righteousness was imparted to us; through Christ, we became one spirit with Him.

We became one with Him! You became just like your Dad! His very DNA became yours. His very genes became yours! That's why you can never say "I can't" or "I'm not good enough." My friend, you are overqualified for everything in life!

A second definition for the word *of* is "to indicate the whole that includes the part denoted by the preceding word." So, according to this definition, if you are "of something," then you are part of it. You and God are one. He became one spirit with us. That's a pretty amazing statement, but it's true because it is Bible. Simply put, whatever God is, you are. Why? Because you are "of Him." When you stepped into Christ, God stepped into you. He put Himself into you. You were born of Him. You are of God!

One last definition for the word *of* is "to indicate belonging or a possessive relationship." So not only do we see that our origin is of God and that we are one with Him, we also see that we belong to Him. We are His possession and I am happy about that! Do you know why? No one takes better care of their belongings than the one who owns them! If God owns me, then I know He will take good care of me! Because I belong to Him, I don't have to worry about a thing.

You are in the greatest hands when you are with God. You are of God my friend, so get excited about it!

<u>**Confession:**</u>
I am of God. My origin is of God. I am one with Him and He is one with me. I can never lack for anything and am overqualified for everything because I am of God!

Day 6

WHAT'S FLOWING OUT OF YOU?

Luke 6:17-19 NLT
When they came down from the mountain, the disciples stood with Jesus on a large, level area, surrounded by many of his followers and by the crowds. There were people from all over Judea and from Jerusalem and from as far north as the seacoasts of Tyre and Sidon. They had come to hear him and to be healed of their diseases; and those troubled by evil spirits were healed. Everyone tried to touch him, because healing power went out from him, and he healed everyone.

Healing power was flowing out of Jesus. My question is, "What is flowing out of you?" Are you expecting to walk as He walked? Are you expecting the same signs and wonders to occur in your life? Do you expect the power of God to flow out of you? You can if it is in you! If you are a believer, full of the Holy Ghost, that healing power, that eternal life is in you! Jesus said we would do the same works that He did and even greater works.

We see this same situation reoccur with Peter in Acts 5. It says that as Peter walked by, people tried to get near his shadow and they were healed. Well, it wasn't his shadow that was healing people (there is no life in darkness). No, it was the glory of God! It was the life of God emanating from Peter's body.

The same thing happened with Paul. In Acts 19, it says that wonderful miracles happened because the power of God was transferred from Paul's body into cloths and those cloths were placed on the sick.

You can expect power to flow from you. The very same life that is in Jesus is in you. The very same Holy Spirit He was anointed with is in you. You are just as righteous, just as sanctified and are carrying the same power. You are the temple of the Holy Ghost, a carrier of the power of Heaven. You need to know what is within you and expect it to come out when released by faith!

It is up to you and I to manifest the power of God. We are to reveal Him and His goodness to the world (and sadly, to most of the modern day Church as well.) Preach the Word and demonstrate the power. When you know, it will flow!

Confession:
I have the life of God in me. That life is transferable and it flows out of my body. When I expect it to flow out of me and the receiver expects it to flow out of me, the life of God, that healing power flows like rivers of living water! I expect to be used by God and used in miraculous ways.

Day 7

WHAT'S IN YOUR HOLSTER?

John 5:43 AMP
I have come in My Father's name and with His power...

Have you ever noticed how bold Jesus was? Jesus was not some wimpy little weenie; Jesus was a man's man. Everywhere He went, He exuded confidence. Jesus was extremely confident and bold because He knew what He possessed.

When I was in college, I had a friend who delivered medical supplies to home bound patients. One day he had to go into the 5th ward of Houston. If you don't know about Houston's 5th ward, let me tell you something – parts of it are an extremely rough and dangerous place.

Well, my friend drove into these particular projects in the 5th ward and starting getting the packages out of the van. As he was walking past some of the houses to get to the home bound patient, he noticed this large man across the street wearing a long overcoat. At that moment, the man opened the overcoat and revealed a sawed off shotgun. Now my friend was a pretty big guy and could handle himself in a fight, but he knew he had nothing to defend himself with, especially against a sawed off shotgun. As they say on the streets, that man was packing some serious heat - and my friend had nothing but a cell phone. Needless to say, my buddy dropped off the package and got out of there quick.

What made that man stand there so boldly and confidently? What made my friend know that man meant business? Because that man was packing some serious heat! You don't mess with a weapon like that! That dude didn't have to say a word; all he did was show his power.

Well, what do you do when Satan opens his overcoat and reveals his trials and tests? What do you do when he reveals his sickness and disease? I tell you what I do! I pull the power of God out of my holster! When Satan shows his ugly head, you let him know real quick, "I stand here in the name of Jesus and with His power!" I tell you, I've got more power in my pinky than all the power of hell put together!

You don't have to be a Barney Fife one bullet wonder. You are loaded with power. The same Power that raised Jesus from the dead is dwelling within you! When I walk in the room, Satan shrinks in terror. Why? Because the power of God just stepped into the room!

Confession:
I have the authority of Jesus and I live, move, and minister with His power. Regardless what comes my way, it is no match for the power of God; therefore, it's no match for me!

Day 8

ALIENS

John 8:23 NKJV
And He said to them, "You are from beneath; I am from above. You are of this world; I am not of this world."

One of the keys to the boldness and confidence we see in Jesus is His understanding of His identity. All throughout the Gospels, we constantly see Jesus talking about who He is, whose He is and where He is from. If Jesus thought and spoke these things about Himself, we certainly should do the same thing.

The truth of Jesus' origin was key in His life. Jesus knew He was a foreigner, an alien in this world. The world's system was not His system. This world's laws were not His laws. Heaven was His home and He was, in a sense, visiting a foreign land on business. Jesus also knew His world was far superior to this earthly world; therefore, He caused the earthly world to come into His subjection whenever the need arose.

When you accepted Jesus as your Lord and Savior, you ceased being a mere man. When you stepped into Christ, you became a God-man and your citizenship was changed. Therefore, look at your circumstances from a different perspective. Look at sickness and disease from a different perspective. Look at finances from a different perspective. This world's system does not dictate how we can live nor what we can do. We are from a different world with different laws that supersede that of this natural world.

I wouldn't suggest going around and telling everyone that you are an alien, but I would suggest that you begin meditating on it! A crucial aspect of the boldness we see Jesus walking in was due to this truth: He was not of this world, but from above. He was ABOVE sickness, ABOVE disease, ABOVE poverty, ABOVE sin, ABOVE addictions, ABOVE everything earthly - and so are you!

Confession:
Heaven is my home. It is where I am from, where I am going and where I am now. I am not from this world, but from above and I operate according to the laws of Heaven. The things of this world do not dictate how I live my life.

Day 9

FILLED TO THE FULL

Colossians 2:10 NKJV
And you are complete in Him who is the head of all principality and power.

Have you ever wondered if you have what it takes to be a successful Christian? Well, stop wondering; you've got the goods.

When you stepped into Christ, you received everything you will ever need. You went from being broken to whole. You went from being sick to healed. You went from being poor to wealthy.

The word *complete* in Colossians 2:10 means "to fill to the top, filled to the full, liberally supplied, to cause to abound." I like that one definition: filled to the full. You know, nothing God gives you is ever "just a little bit." Every time God gives to you, it is always in abundance. When He poured His Spirit into you, He filled you up! When you stepped into Christ, you stepped into all that He is and all that He has. God filled you up to overflowing with Him.

This verse really exposes a great deal of the religious junk that is being fed in many churches today. You aren't trying to get good enough, you aren't trying to get smart enough, and you aren't trying to get anointed enough. You have the fullness of the Godhead in you.

You see, throughout the world, we sing songs like "More love, more power" and yet we have the love of God shed abroad in our hearts and the power source of the world living in us. We have all the love and power Heaven has to offer, but because we haven't realized we are complete in Christ, we sing stupid songs like this.

Satan doesn't want you to know you have it all; he wants you thinking you are lacking. If Satan can convince you that you need more to get the job done, he's got you whipped.

Jesus said "My peace I leave with you." Jesus made us whole; He gave us His wholeness, He made us complete and He expects you to walk in it. You may not think you have it because you aren't seeing it in your life. Well, we don't walk by what we see! It's all within you; you just have to realize you've got it. You are complete in Christ, so walk through life filled to the full.

Confession:
In Christ, I am complete. In Christ, I am lacking nothing. I have everything I need to fulfill all that God has called me to do. Everything Jesus has, I have. His wisdom is mine, His authority is mine, His love is mine, His joy is mine, His strength is mine, and His faith is mine.

Day 10

I AM ANOINTED

Luke 4:17-18 NKJV
And He was handed the book of the prophet Isaiah. And when He had opened the book, He found the place where it was written: "The Spirit of the LORD is upon Me, Because He has anointed Me to preach the gospel to the poor; He has sent Me to heal the brokenhearted, to proclaim liberty to the captives and recovery of sight to the blind, to set at liberty those who are oppressed; to proclaim the acceptable year of the LORD."

This wasn't the first time Jesus read this passage of scripture. He didn't just so happen to flip to the page and start reading; Jesus knew exactly where this passage of scripture was, what it said and what it meant. In other words, Jesus had been reading and meditating on this scripture for a while.

Remember, although He was the Son of God, Jesus was operating on the earth as a man. This meant that He was growing in wisdom, and constantly renewing and maintaining His mind. Therefore, as a man, Jesus had to continually keep His mind on the truth that He was anointed.

Why do we seem to be defeated so many times? We aren't aware of the anointing of God in and upon us. Jesus said in John 14 we would do the same works as Him and even greater works; although, if we are going to do the same works as Christ, we must have the same mindset as Him. We must know that we are anointed too!

What does the anointing do? It removes burdens and destroys yokes. It gets rid of anything standing in your way!

Start reminding yourself and meditating on the truth that you are anointed. That way when a situation arises, you are ready! You won't be afraid, but you will know that you are equipped and empowered for victory!

See yourself in this passage of scripture. Put your name in it and confess it anytime you think about it. For example: The Spirit of the Lord is upon Chad, because He has anointed Chad to preach the Gospel to the poor, He has sent Chad to heal the brokenhearted, to proclaim liberty to the captives and recovery of sight to the blind. God sent Chad to set at liberty those who are oppressed and to proclaim the acceptable year of the Lord!

If doing that doesn't fire you up, you have problems! Shout it with me, "I am anointed!"

Confession:
I am anointed. Everything around me tells me differently, but the Word says it; therefore I believe it. I am equipped. I am empowered by the Holy Spirit to do the works of the Lord! I AM ANOINTED!

Day 11

GIVE SOME LIFE AWAY

John 4:10 NKJV
Jesus answered and said to her, "If you knew the gift of God and Who it is Who says to you, 'Give Me a drink,' you would have asked Him and He would have given you living water."

Jesus knew Who He was and the authority that He possessed; He also knew the gift that He possessed – that gift was eternal life. During one of Jesus' conversations with the disciples, He told them that not only did He possess the life of God, but he also had the authority to give it away.

We also see throughout Jesus' earthly ministry that anyone who was in need of God's life and asked in faith always received. What is this life? It is the Greek word zoe which is the very life and nature of God. It's the life which caused and upholds life for all creation; the same life which also destroys sickness, disease and raises the dead.

The key point to John 4:10 is that not only did Jesus possess it, but He was also able to give it away. When you accepted Christ as your Lord and Savior, you became a possessor of life as well. Not only did you become a possessor of life, but you also became a dispenser of it! There are people all around you that need an outpouring of God's life in their bodies and spirit. God needs you to reach out and touch someone!

Remember the story in Acts 3 of Peter, John and the lame man? Notice what Peter said, "What I have I give unto you!" Well, you can't give away what you don't have. What did Peter give away? Life! Eternal, abundant, God infused life! Peter put a dose of life into the man's legs and he then began to run and jump! Peter knew what he possessed and he gave some away.

Be conscious of the life of God within you. Stop being stingy and give some life away!

Confession:
I am a possessor of the life and nature of God. What I possess, I can give away. When the life of God is needed in a situation, I choose to be used. I am a dispenser of life. I am a minister of life. I purpose to be used and to give life to those who need it.

Day 12

DISPENSERS

2 Corinthians 3:6 AMP
[It is He] Who has qualified us [making us to be fit and worthy and sufficient] as ministers and dispensers of a new covenant [of salvation through Christ], not [ministers] of the letter (of legally written code) but of the Spirit; for the code [of the Law] kills, but the [Holy] Spirit makes alive.

God called us to not only speak His Word, but also to demonstrate it with action. Notice in our text that we are to be dispensers of the New Covenant, dispensers of the Spirit. What all does the New Covenant entail? Freedom from sickness, freedom from disease, freedom from poverty, and freedom from spiritual death; basically, a release from Satan's bondage! We've been preaching it, but we haven't been dispensing it!

You must see this! We've been sitting back waiting on God and wondering where the miracles have been. Yet, we see the answer to our problem right here in 2 Cor 3:6. We've been waiting on God to dispense the life, but He made us the dispensers! God already poured His Spirit into us so we could pour His Spirit on others!

If people want to be free, you have what it takes to make them free; you have the Almighty Spirit of God within you! I jokingly refer to the childhood song, "I'm A Little Teapot." I changed it up

29

just a tiny bit and sing it like this: "I'm a big teapot short and stout, here is my handle, here is my spout. Tip me over and pour Life out; sickness and disease, you better watch out!" (I know it's a little cheesy, but it helps get the point across.)

Think about yourself as a walking, living pitcher or dispenser - almost like the Kool-Aid man! Wherever you go, you are a vessel and carrier of the life of God. You are filled to the full with life! So let's take ministry a step further- act like God is in you and pour Him out!

Confession:
God has made me a dispenser of His new covenant. He has made me a dispenser of His Spirit. God poured His Spirit into me so I can pour His Spirit onto others!

Day 13

MASTERS

Romans 6:6 NKJV
We know that our old (unrenewed) self was nailed to the cross with Him in order that [our] body [which is the instrument] of sin might be made ineffective and inactive for evil, that we might no longer be the slaves of sin.

Sin and everything associated with it is never to dominate us; we are to dominate it. Because of our position in Christ, now WE DOMINATE SIN AND WE DOMINATE SICKNESS. Satan is no longer our master, he is now our slave; when we speak in the Name of Jesus by faith, Satan's only response is 'Yes sir, whatever you say sir."

We are masters of sin. We are masters of sickness. We are masters over our emotions. We are masters over addiction. Addictions have no control over us. You can never say, "Well, I just can't help it!" because if you do, you are a liar. You can help it because of who you are in Christ.

Addiction may have a hold in our body and mind, but not our spirit. You take your authority and your seated position next to the Throne and tell sin what it can do. You tell your mind and your body what to do because you are a master; you are a king in this life!

31

Don't let Satan dominate you. Don't allow yourself to feel like you have no control and that you are helpless. Outside of Christ, you didn't have much choice; inside Christ, you have a choice! Before Christ, you were under Satan's feet; after Christ, Satan is under your feet.

You aren't Satan's slave anymore; there is no slave sitting at the right hand of God! You're Satan's master! Sin and sickness no longer controls you!

Confession:
I am a master over sin, sickness and disease. Because I am in Christ and seated at the right hand of God, I tell sin and sickness what to do. I no longer have to submit to the pressures of sin; now sin and sickness submit to my orders. When I tell them to go...they go...and they go now!

Day 14

EIGHT PERCENT

Matthew 14:28-29 NKJV
And Peter answered Him and said, "Lord, if it is You, command me to come to You on the water." So He said, "Come." And when Peter had come down out of the boat, he walked on the water to go to Jesus.

Why is it we don't see much of the power of God being displayed? Why is much of Christianity placing the miracle working power of God in the past? It is simply because there are only a few of us working it and not too many people are seeing it!

When Peter stepped out on the water, the rest of the disciples could have followed, but they simply sat in awe. If they were like most Christians today, they would be thinking, "Man, that Peter must have a real special anointing on his life." No, Peter was just like them - same equipment, same ability - he simply was bold enough to step out. Of the twelve disciples, 8% stepped out and worked the supernatural.

In the parable of the Sower in Mark 4, we find the same statistics. Only 25% of the people actually received something; 8% total actually dared to get all God had for them - only 8% received 100% of what God made available.

What does this all mean? It's time to step out! It's time to start acting like a believer! It's time to stop waiting and start walking!

Only 8% of us are walking on the water; the other 92% of the Church is sitting complacently in the boat twiddling their thumbs and waiting on a move of God. 8% of the Church is making a move; the other 92% are waiting on a move.

You are a supernatural being with supernatural authority and supernatural power - now start acting like it. Be part of the elite group, the special forces of the Church!

Confession:
I will no longer sit back waiting; I am going to start walking. The power of God has been made available to me to use at my disposal. The supernatural is natural to me! The world will know the power of God through me because I am a miracle working machine.

Day 15

YOU ARE A GIFT

2 Corinthians 6:16 AMP
What agreement [can there be between] a temple of God and idols? For we are the temple of the living God; even as God said, I will dwell in and with and among them and will walk in and with and among them, and I will be their God, and they shall be My people.

So many of us are waiting on a move of God; we are waiting on a manifestation before we do anything. We are waiting for a gift of the Spirit to show up before we take even the slightest step.

When God moved into us, we became a move. When we became one with Christ, we became a gift to the world. Quite simply, wherever you are, no matter what the situation you are in, you have everything it takes to get the job done.

Am I saying that we are independent of God? No way! We are fully dependent on Him; yet, I am trying to emphasize our unity with God. For some reason, we haven't gotten it yet, but we are going to now. In Christ, we are complete! You are not lacking anything, but we must realize who we are, who we are one with and start walking in it.

We've got the goods my friends! You've been called, appointed, equipped and anointed. You are a gift. Because the Holy Ghost lives in you, when you show up, YOU BRING THE GIFT - and He has everything you need.

<u>Confession:</u>
I am a gift to the world. The Holy Spirit lives in me; therefore, when I show up, everything I need is already there. When I arrive on the scene, the gifts of Heaven arrive on the scene. All of Heaven is at my disposal to get the job done. I am complete in Christ.

Day 16

THE GOSPEL OF DEMONSTRATION

1 Corinthians 2:4, 5 NKJV
And my speech and my preaching were not with persuasive words of human wisdom, but in demonstration of the Spirit and of power, that your faith should not be in the wisdom of men but in the power of God.

Do you realize the Gospel is a message of power? Although, go to most churches and you won't see anything - that's why most people don't go to church anymore. The world is looking for the power in all the wrong places because the Church isn't demonstrating it. The world is calling psychic hotlines, going to hypnotists and playing around with witchcraft because they are hungry for the power. Whether you are saved or not, you are still a spirit being and we have a natural craving for supernatural things.

God never intended for us to preach His Message without confirmation of that Message. Do you remember what happened after Jesus gave the great commission? The Bible says, "And the disciples went preaching everywhere, the Lord working with them, confirming the Word with signs, wonders and miracles." (Mark 16:20) God was demonstrating the power! He was confirming that the disciples' message was true.

You may say, "Yeah, but we are to walk by faith, not by sight."

Well, that may be true, but the world walks by sight. The world wants to see the power; they need to see it!

Did you ever notice how many times Jesus referred to the "works of God" or the miracles which He performed? Do you remember when He said, "If you don't believe what I say, believe what I do?" Why would He say that? Because people may not believe the message that God is the Healer, but when you impart God's power into a blind person and they begin seeing...YOU WILL GET THEIR ATTENTION. As a result, they will be open to hear what you have to say. Actions speak louder than words!

Be determined not to preach a powerless gospel. Expect God to confirm the Message you preach. Expect God to work through you. Demonstrate the power and make believers out of the world. If you want to get a convert, give them the word, step out and expect God to demonstrate. Remember, God is in you and He backs up His Word. You don't need a fancy word...you have a fancy God!

<u>Confession:</u>
God is the Demonstrator. When I speak His Word, He backs it up! He confirms it! I will be obedient in allowing God to work through me.

Day 17

LIVING OUT OF HEAVEN

John 3:13 AMP
And yet no one has ever gone up to Heaven, but there is
One Who has come down from Heaven- the Son of Man
[Himself], Who is (dwells, has His home) in Heaven.

It sounds a little strange that Jesus would be standing on the earth
talking to men and women and yet say that He was in Heaven. If you
didn't know any better, you would think He was nuts! Imagine if you
are a native of Texas and you go to visit some friends in Oklahoma.
During your conversation, you say, "Yeah, I am from Texas and
that's where I am right now." Your friends would think you were
out of your mind. They would say, "How is that possible if you are
physically here in Oklahoma?"

The wonderful thing about Jesus was that his physical body may
have been on the earth, but His thoughts were on Heaven. He may
have been amongst the problems of this world, but He was living out
of Heaven. Jesus understood that physically He was on the earth, but
positionally He was still in Heaven - for that is where He was living
and ministering from. This is one of the key reasons why Jesus was
a master of His circumstances.

So what about you and I? Ephesians 2 tells us that we are seated at God's right hand and that we are citizens of Heaven. Physically we are on this earth, but positionally, we are in Heaven. That is why we have access to all of Heaven's resources.

In a sense, Jesus walked with one foot in the natural and one foot in the supernatural. His thoughts were always on Heavenly things. His mind was always on higher things - that is why He walked above everything.

<u>Confession:</u>
I am a citizen of Heaven. Heaven is where I am from, where I am going and positionally, it is where I am right now!

Day 18

BE A BELIEVER TODAY

John 14:12 NKJV
Most assuredly, I say to you, he who believes in Me, the works that I do he will do also; and greater works than these he will do, because I go to My Father.

Mark 16:17-19 NIV
And these signs will accompany those who believe: In my name they will drive out demons; they will speak in new tongues; they will pick up snakes with their hands; and when they drink deadly poison, it will not hurt them at all; they will place their hands on sick people, and they will get well.

The vast majority of the Church believes these verses are in the Bible, but they wouldn't dare act on them. Why? The vast majority of Christians don't believe them.

For the average Joe Christian, these scriptures only apply to preachers – and that's if they even believe these scriptures are applicable today! But where does it say in these two passages of scripture you have to be in full-time ministry? Where does it say you have to pastor a 20,000 member church? Where does it say you have to have a worldwide television ministry? It doesn't! The only qualification that is needed: be a believer.

The following statement is very common: "Well, I'm saved. I'm a believer, but I just don't know about all that." Whoever heard of a believer who didn't believe?

One of my favorite cartoon characters has always been Tigger. I love Tigger because he was always confident in his abilities. One thing Tigger knew he could do was bounce; he would always say, "Bouncing is what Tiggers do best!"

Are you a believer? Well, are you a Christian? If so, then you are a believer and believing is what believers do best!

There was an old secular song called "I'm A Believer." One line says "And I saw her face...now I'm a believer." What if we changed it around: "And I heard the Word...now I'm a believer!"

Believe that what Jesus said is true. Believe that the Holy Ghost is working mightily in you today! Believe that you are a son of God! Decide today you are going to act like a Christian. Decide today you are going to be what you were made to be: a believer! Now go out there and kick the devil's butt!

Confession:
I am a believer. If Jesus said it, then it is true. If Jesus did it on this earth, then I can do it too. Opening blind eyes and deaf ears is normal for me. Seeing the lame jump out of wheel chairs is natural for me. When I walk into a room, devils begin to tremble - because a Christian just walked in.

Day 19

LET GOD ACT OUT

Mark 16:20 NIV
Then the disciples went out and preached everywhere, and the Lord worked with them and confirmed his word by the signs that accompanied it.

We as the Church have sat back and wondered, "Why isn't God doing anything?" "Where are the miracles?" "Where are the wonders?" Well, there is a tremendous clue found in Mark 16:20.

Take notice of our verse. They were first preaching the Word. The Word that we speak and act on is what the Lord has to work with. Mark 16:20 could be read, "...the Lord working with the Word and confirming the Word..."

The Word must be declared and acted on for the confirmation of that Word to take place. If you aren't seeing anything, it's because you aren't saying anything! If you want to start seeing some things, then you need to open your mouth!

When we act on the Word, it gives God something to work with and He will always confirm His Word. When the Word goes forth, it will always accomplish the mission on which it was sent.

It's not up to us to confirm the Word; it's not up to us to make the Word work. Although, it is up to us to act on the Word so that God can act on our actions and show His Word to be true. If you don't act out, God can't act out. Take a step of faith! Step way out there with nothing under your feet but the Word and let God show out big time!

Confession:
I am bold in the Word. I believe that the Word is true. I expect when I speak the Word and when I act on the Word that the Word is always confirmed and shown to be true in my life. From this day forward, miracles are normal for me!

Day 20

TEAM MIRACLE

John 5:17 NKJV
But Jesus answered them, "My Father has been working until now, and I have been working."

Jesus made this statement right after He healed the man at the pool of Bethesda. The religious people were furious at Jesus because He healed someone on the Sabbath; Jesus responded by saying that He and God were working together.

Jesus was trying to help them understand that He and the Father were One. It wasn't just God doing a miracle and it wasn't just Jesus doing a miracle; they were working together as a team. Jesus understood that it wasn't just Him at work; Jesus knew He couldn't do it by Himself.

Jesus was operating as a man anointed by God and God was working through Jesus. That's why Jesus said, "If you see Me, you have seen the Father." Jesus was a partner on God's team; Jesus needed God and God needed Jesus.

You see, God rarely works alone; He made man to work alongside Him. Look at how God treated Adam. God created Adam in His likeness and then involved Adam in Creation.

All throughout history, God has always involved mankind to help in the miracle process. We are co-laborers together with God; we work together as a team.

Know your role on the team. If you don't know your role, you'll be sitting on the bench waiting for some action to come your way – and you know that as long as you are on the bench, you will not be seeing any action.

Your role is the believer; God's role is the Performer. Your job is to step out in faith and initiate the miracle. You start it and God will always finish it!

Confession:
When I am working the works of Jesus, God is always working with me. I am never alone for God is always with me and working through me. I am a member of God's miracle team!

Day 21

THE STANDARD

Matthew 11:2-5 NLT
John the Baptist, who was in prison, heard about all the things the Messiah was doing. So he sent his disciples to ask Jesus, "Are you the Messiah we've been expecting, or should we keep looking for someone else?" Jesus told them, "Go back to John and tell him what you have heard and seen - the blind see, the lame walk, the lepers are cured, the deaf hear, the dead are raised to life, and the Good News is being preached to the poor."

When the validity of Jesus' ministry came into question, Jesus always referred to the miracles He worked. Actions speak louder than words and Jesus knew it. Jesus told the people, "If you don't believe what I say, believe what I do." Jesus is the standard for ministry and the Christian life. We are telling people, "Didn't you hear what was said?" when we should be saying, "Didn't you see what was done?"

Paul tells us in Romans that all of creation is waiting for the sons of God to be revealed. How will the world know that the sons of God are here? Signs, wonders and miracles. How did the people know Jesus was the Son of God? They knew by the works that He did.

The Bible is being preached all across the world by TV, internet, radio, DVD, mp3, books and CD; yet, statistics indicate that many of the world wants nothing to do with the Church. We are in a day and age where the Church is known more for entertainment, affairs and money scandals than we are the miraculous.

It's time we get back to the standard Jesus set for the Church. Do we want the world to listen to us once again? Do we want our governments to look to us once again? Then we must give them something to see. There will be some who will still not believe, but when they do see, decisions will have to be made. It's time to raise our standard to the one Jesus set; it's time to manifest the power of God. If you want to see the miraculous happening in your church or ministry, start declaring what Jesus declared.

We've been doing this in our ministry since its inception. Tell people that at your church, the blind see, the lame walk, the diseased are cured, the deaf hear, the dead are raised and the good news is preached! Even if you haven't seen anything in the past, get ready... because you are raising the standard and speaking words of faith; you are opening the doorway to the miraculous!

<u>Confession:</u>
I am a believer of Christ. I am one with Him. Therefore, I will make the blind to see, the lame to walk, the diseased to be cured, the deaf to hear, and the dead to be raised. People will see the power of God through me.

Day 22

AS GOD TO PHARAOH

Exodus 7:1 NIV
Then the Lord said to Moses, "See, I have made you like God
to Pharaoh, and your brother Aaron will be your prophet."

This is one of the most astounding statements in the Bible. The
first time I ever saw this, I had to pick my jaw up off the floor; I
thought I had misread this scripture! I read it again and I began to
see the significance of this wonderful verse.

God had a plan for Moses to deliver the Israelites. Once Moses
was informed, he starts making excuses as to why he can't get the
job done. At the end of Exodus 6, Moses explains that he is not a
good speaker; yet, God responds with this tremendous statement in
Exodus 7:1, "I have made you as God to Pharaoh." In other words,
Moses had God's ability to get the job done because he was God's
representative. Moses could do the job just as well as if it was God
doing it Himself on the earth.

Notice the phrase *as God*. Moses wasn't God; although, on the
earth, God had equipped Moses with His ability to totally fulfill the
call on his life. Moses had been given authority and power over
Pharaoh and God expected him to use it.

Now let's think about this. If God gave Moses, an unsaved man living under the Old Covenant, this type of authority and power on the earth – how much more has He given the child of God?

The question is, "What is the Pharaoh in your life?" Is it poverty, sickness, depression or addictions? Whatever it is that is trying to hold you in bondage, you have been made as God to it. God has given you the ability to whip Pharaoh's tail!

You are a master on this earth; to put it bluntly, you are a god on this earth and you were made to work the miraculous. Look at Moses' life; it was a life full of the miraculous! He parted the Red Sea and even caused water to come out of a rock – twice!

What about the believer? It's time to realize who we truly are. We've been made as God to the pharaohs of this world; it's time to let the signs, wonders and miracles loose!

Confession:
God has made me His representative on this earth. God has given me the authority and power to fulfill His plans, purposes and pursuits on the earth! The miraculous is normal for me.

Day 23

YOU DO IT

Exodus 14:15-16 NKJV
And the Lord said to Moses, "Why do you cry to Me? Tell the children of Israel to go forward. But lift up your rod, stretch out your hand over the sea and divide it..."

Is God is withholding the power? No, the problem has been due to a case of spineless Christianity. We want God to do something, but God requires us to do something. Most of the Church has lost all sense of boldness and courage; we have lost our sense of responsibility. We don't want to step out for fear of damaging our reputation.

As Moses stands before the Red Sea, He makes a great faith statement in verses 13-14. Yet, as great as the statement was, Moses had forgotten about God's statement to him in Exodus 7:1, "See, I have made you as God." God tells Moses that he is to stretch out his hand and he is to divide the sea.

Do you see it? God says, "Moses, why are you putting this off on me. I have given you the authority and ability to act on my behalf in the earth and get the same results I would. Now Moses, act like me - you divide it!"

We have more of a part to play on this earth than we realize.

The signs, wonders, and miracles are not a thing of the past; they are always for the present. If we haven't been seeing anything, it's because we haven't been working anything.

Remember what Jesus said in Mark 11:23-24? He was talking about a mountain being in your way. Notice He didn't tell us to pray for God to move it; He tells us to move it. How? Speak to it!

Jesus didn't tell us to ask God's permission because God has already given us permission to destroy those things that bind and hinder our lives. If something is hindering, blocking or holding us back from fulfilling God's plan, we are to use the authority God has given to us. In a sense, what God told Moses in Exodus 7 and 14 is what Jesus was telling us in Mark 11. USE THE FAITH OF GOD! Let God work through you! Stop waiting on God; you do it and He'll back you up!

Confession:
I have the authority and ability of God on this earth to act on His behalf. If a mountain is in my way, I speak to it. If the winds of life blow my way, I speak to it. If the impossible stands before me, I'll step out and work a miracle. I'm not waiting anymore; I'm going forward and living in the miraculous.

Day 24

DISOBEDIENT MIRACLES

Numbers 20: 11 NLT
Then Moses raised his hand and struck the rock twice with the staff, and water gushed out. So all the people and their livestock drank their fill.

This is one of the most amazing passages of scripture. What an amazing miracle! Moses hits a rock twice and causes water to come out. It wasn't just a trickle of water either, but enough to take care of millions of people and animals. What is more amazing is that Moses performed this miracle in disobedience.

In Numbers 20:8, God told Moses, "You and Aaron must take the staff and assemble the entire community. As the people watch, command the rock over there to pour out its water. You will get enough water from the rock to satisfy all the people and their livestock." Moses was supposed to speak to the rock, not hit the rock. This act of disobedience cost Moses the opportunity to go into the Promised Land.

So what is the significance of this? Even in disobedience, Moses still worked a miracle. Moses was so confident in his authority as God's representative, Moses did it his way and still got it to work. Absolutely amazing! Was Moses wrong in disobeying God? Yes. Although, it gives us a glimpse into the authority Moses was walking in and the very minimum of what we should be walking in.

How much more authority should we be walking in as children of God? Moses wasn't saved. He wasn't seated at God's right hand. He didn't have the Holy Spirit residing in him; yet, he was so confident in God's presence and his authority - even in disobedience, He worked a mighty, mighty miracle.

Confession:
Because I am a child of God, I have authority. The authority Moses walked in pales in comparison to what I have. When I speak, the things of this world listen. All authority has been given to me and I purpose to walk in it!

Day 25

SAME JOB, SAME RESULTS

John 14:12 NKJV
Most assuredly, I say to you, he who believes in Me, the works
that I do he will do also; and greater works than these he will
do, because I go to My Father.

Jesus told us if we believed in Him, we would do the same works
that He did. Well, what were those works? Acts 10:38 tells us that
Jesus went around doing good and healing all those who were
oppressed by the devil. If you read the Gospels, you readily see that
healing was one of the great works Jesus did.

My question to you is this: are you a believer? If you answered
yes, then you qualify to do the same works as Jesus! Healing is
for today and there are millions around the world (even in your
neighborhood) that need God's healing power. You could pray
for God to touch their life or you could stand up in your authority as
a believer and touch them for yourself!

Don't ever think that you can't do the works Jesus did; He just
told us in John 14:12 that we could! Why? Because Jesus went to
the Father so He could send us the Holy Spirit; the Holy Spirit will
help bring those things to pass if you will simply act on His Word.
These works are even part of the Great Commission; remember, we

are to preach the Gospel and demonstrate the Gospel – part of that is healing the sick! You aren't the Savior and you aren't the Healer, but the Savior and the Healer is working in and through you.

You can do the same works and get the same results. Remember all those blind and deaf people Jesus healed? Remember the lame people Jesus healed? Remember the lepers Jesus healed? Remember the dead people Jesus raised? You can do those same works if you just believe!

Confession:
Healing is for me. It is not only for me to partake of, it is also for me to give away because I am a believer. I can do what Jesus did and get the very same results; therefore, I will do the works of Jesus and I will get the very same results!

Day 26

GET YOUR FEET WET

Joshua 3:13-16 NIV
"And as soon as the priests who carry the ark of the LORD -the Lord of all the earth—set foot in the Jordan, its waters flowing downstream will be cut off and stand up in a heap." So when the people broke camp to cross the Jordan, the priests carrying the Ark of the Covenant went ahead of them. Now the Jordan is at flood stage all during harvest. Yet as soon as the priests who carried the ark reached the Jordan and their feet touched the water's edge, the water from upstream stopped flowing...

For the miraculous to occur, one needs to be willing to get his feet wet. To see the miraculous in your life, you have to be willing to take a step of faith. Go to the edge of what you can do and then watch God take over. The Jordan River didn't part until the priests got into the water; they had to go to the limits of what they could do.

God always requires us to be active participants! When it seems that the situation is impossible, that's when you need to step out in faith. I think it's great how God points out that the Jordan was at flood stage. What was an impossible situation was now even worse; but God required some faith.

You see, we are co-laborers together with God. God wants you to do what you cannot do in the natural. Look at Jesus; a number of the healings that took place in His ministry were a result of the sick person doing something they couldn't do. When they stepped out in faith, a miracle transpired. They were participating in the miracle process! Do the impossible and allow God to make it possible!

Confession:
I work together with God and that's why the miraculous is normal for me. When I step out in faith, God always backs me up. I don't step out because of what I see; I step out because of what I believe.

Day 27

DO THE IMPOSSIBLE TO SEE THE IMPOSSIBLE

John 9:1, 6-7 NLT
As Jesus was walking along, he saw a man who had been blind from birth. Then he spit on the ground, made mud with the saliva, and spread the mud over the blind man's eyes. He told him, "Go wash yourself in the pool of Siloam" (Siloam means "sent"). So the man went and washed and came back seeing!

Here's a big question for you. How does a blind man find a pool of water by himself? It almost seems uncompassionate for Jesus to tell someone who can't see to go wash his eyes in a pool of water. After all, the guy can't see! So how is he supposed to find the water? Quite simply - by faith!

Jesus knew how to get a miracle. Jesus was a master at getting people into a position to receive by faith! Jesus knew the strong relationship between faith and obedience. When the blind man walked away from Jesus, he was walking toward his miracle.

If you want to see the impossible, you must be willing to do the impossible. With God all things are possible, but it begins by you initiating something with your faith.

In the natural, Jesus told the blind man to do something that seemed pretty unreasonable; but, it made the blind man step out in faith! You know that for an instant, the blind man had to have thought this was crazy; thankfully, he was smart enough to keep his mouth shut and start walking!

He had probably been in that water plenty of times and nothing had happened. Yet, it wasn't some magical water that healed the man; it was his faith shown by his obedience to the Word of God.

His obedience to the Word, although the act seemed a little foolish, produced the needed result. If God says it and you act on it - get ready, because you are about to see the impossible become possible!

Confession:
If the Word says it, I will do it. Regardless if it doesn't make sense to my mind, I will always obey the Word and as a result, the impossible will become possible!

Day 28

ZAPPED

2 Samuel 6:6, 7 NLT
But when they arrived at the threshing floor of Nacon, the oxen stumbled, and Uzzah reached out his hand and steadied the Ark of God. Then the Lord's anger was aroused against Uzzah, and God struck him dead because of this. So Uzzah died right there beside the Ark of God.

Can you imagine the power that must have been within the Ark of God? When Uzzah reached out and touched the ark, He died instantly. Why? Number one, the ark of God was holy and Uzzah was not. In other words, if anything unholy touched the ark of God, it died instantly. Where life is, death can not survive!

Secondly, the ark of God was full of God Himself! Wherever the ark went, the power and presence of God went as well. Do you see where I am going with this?

Because of Jesus' sacrifice, the Bible says that God moved out of the box and moved into you. Now you are the vessel of God! So, when sickness tries to touch you, it should get zapped like a bug touching a bug zapper. Death can not survive when it touches the life of God. The flu should think twice about stopping by your house for a visit because it knows what is inside!

If the power of God is residing within you, then you need to stop asking, praying, and singing for more power! You have all the power you need for any situation that may come your way. You have the Holy Spirit within you!

When people come to you for healing, tell them to get prepared because when you lay your hands on them, the juice is coming loose; they are about to get zapped!

<u>Confession:</u>
By the Holy Spirit, God resides within me. If God is in me, then His power is in me. Sickness and disease are no match for me. I'm a disease zapper! I'm a sickness zapper! When demons come around, I zap them too!

Day 29

HOLY GHOST JUMPER CABLES

Luke 4:40 NIV
When the sun was setting, the people brought to Jesus all who had various kinds of sickness, and laying his hands on each one, he healed them.

Some may say, "Well that worked for Jesus, but that won't work for me." Says who? Ever read your Bible?

If it's flowing through Christ and you are in Christ, it's flowing through you! He's the Vine and you are the branch; if He's got it, then you've got it because you and Christ are unified!

Do you realize what happens when you place your hands on someone in faith for healing? You release healing power! You release the abundant, eternal, zoe life of God. The power of God flows from your spirit into the body of the diseased person and zaps them with life!

Most of us have experienced the battery in our vehicle being dead. So if you have a dead battery, what do you do? You need to impart some life. How is that accomplished? Well, you need two things: a battery with life and some jumper cables. You place one end of the jumper cables on the live battery and the other end of the jumper cables on the dead battery. As a result, life gets transmitted.

It works the same with healing power! You are full of the life of God, a dispenser of glory, and anointed from on High. We are supernatural beings with a direct connection to Heaven.

It's like placing one hand on the Throne of God and placing the other hand on the sick person. In faith, you transmit life! Your hands are holy hands! Your hands are miracle working hands! Your hands are Holy Ghost jumper cables!

When you lay hands on the sick, don't do it hoping something happens. Know that you are hooked up to something that can knock them out of their shoes! You must believe that you are connected to a live battery and there is something about to flow through you and cause a miracle to take place.

Get ready for the electricity of God to flow! Get ready to transmit the power and glory of God.

Confession:
I am hooked up to the Source of life and power. When I lay hands on the sick, they better get ready to receive, because I have something to give. My hands are Holy Ghost jumper cables hooked up to the Throne of God. When I lay hands on the sick, they will be made whole!

Day 30

IF YOU SAW HIM DO IT,
YOU CAN DO IT TOO

John 5:19 AMP
So Jesus answered them by saying, I assure you, most solemnly I tell you, the Son is able to do nothing of Himself (of His own accord); but He is able to do only what He sees the Father doing, for whatever the Father does is what the Son does in the same way [in His turn].

This is a powerful statement for the Christian to live by. Not only does it show us why Jesus did what He did, but it also shows why we can do the works of Jesus.

So many times we disqualify ourselves because we think Jesus did the miraculous due to His being God. It is true that Jesus is part of the Trinity and 100% God, but on the earth, He was operating 100% as a man. In Philippians 2:7, we see that Jesus stripped Himself of His Godly privileges; He was a Man allowing God to work through Him – just like you and I. Notice what Jesus said, "I am able to do nothing in and of myself; it's God doing the work through Me." Jesus was dependent upon God's ability flowing through Him.

If all the miracles and all the supernatural works were done by the Man Jesus, what does that say about you? What does that say about me? I am a man and I am a son of God. Well, that must mean

I can do just what Jesus did!

Remember what Jesus said in John 14:12? He said, "He who believes in Me will do the same works that I do and even greater works." Well, I am a believer, so count me in!

Notice also that Jesus did what He saw God do; therefore, we are to do what we see Jesus do. Isn't He our example? We are to imitate Him and be just like Him!

We can't work the miraculous in and of ourselves, but we can work the miraculous because of Who is on the inside of us! Glory to God! I am one with Christ and He is one with me. I am one with God and He is one with me! I have the same Holy Ghost working in and upon me that Jesus did on this earth. I am wholly dependent on God and I am determined to allow Him to work through me.

Confession:
Jesus worked the miraculous as a Man wholly dependent on God. Jesus said I could do what He did, so I determine from this day forward to be a miracle worker. Miracles are normal for me because God lives and works through me!

NOTES

NOTES

NOTES

NOTES

NOTES

ABOUT THE AUTHOR

Chad holds a M.Ed. in Counseling from Lamar University and a D.Min. from School of Bible Theology and Seminary University.

With an emphasis on one's union with Christ, Dr. Chad Gonzales brings a powerful and practical message of faith and grace to the world. The mission of Chad Gonzales Ministries is to connect people to God so they can manifest God to their world. Declaring the Gospel with simplicity, boldness and humor, mighty miracles of healing are common in their meetings.

Together with their son Jake, Chad and Lacy minister around the world teaching and proving that Jesus loves, Jesus heals and Jesus wants to work through you!

OTHER BOOKS AVAILABLE BY THE AUTHOR

Aliens
An Alternate Reality
Believing God For A House
Eight Percent
Fearless
God's Will Is You Healed
Making Right Decisions
Naturally Supernatural
The Freedom of Forgiveness
Think Like Jesus
Walking In The Miraculous
What's Next

The Supernatural Life Podcast

Check out *The Supernatural Life Podcast with Chad Gonzales!*
New episodes are available each month designed to help you connect
with God on a deeper level and live the supernatural life God desires
for you to have.

The Healing Academy is an outreach of Chad Gonzales Ministries to help the everyday believer learn to walk according to the standard of Jesus in the ministry of healing.

Jesus said in John 14:12 that whoever believes in Him would do the same works and even greater works. Through *The Healing Academy*, it is our goal to raise the standard of the healing ministry in the Church up to the standard of Jesus Himself and manifest the ministry of Jesus in the marketplace.

The Healing Academy is available by video training series as well as in person training. For more information, please visit :

www.ChadGonzales.com

SALVATION AND THE BAPTISM
OF THE HOLY SPIRIT

Dear friend, it is the desire of God that everyone accepts His free gift of salvation. God sent the greatest gift Heaven had so the world could be set free; that precious gift was Jesus! Despite knowing the mistakes you would make, He died for you anyway. Jesus knew the mistakes you would make, yet He still climbed up on the cross. Why? His love was greater than your sin.

Romans 10:9-10 says if you will confess Jesus as your Lord and Savior and believe that He arose from the dead, you will be saved. You see, salvation has nothing to do with works. It doesn't matter what church you belong to, how many little old ladies you help across the street or how much you give the church. You cannot earn salvation; you cannot buy salvation; you must simply accept salvation.

Another free gift that God has provided is the Baptism of the Holy Spirit. In Acts 2, we find the Baptism of the Holy Spirit being given to the Church. God desires that you be filled with His Spirit with the evidence of speaking in tongues.

God said in Acts 2:38 that this life changing gift was for everyone, not just a select few. It wasn't just for those living in Bible days; it was given to everyone who would accept Jesus as Lord and Savior. Jesus said the purpose of the Baptism of the Holy Spirit was so you could be a witness with power! You'll find that when you receive the Baptism of the Holy Spirit, it allows you to operate in the fullness of God's power and be a blessing to the entire world. Essentially, you could say that salvation gets you into a relationship with God and the

Baptism of the Holy Spirit helps you get others into a relationship with God.

Regardless of who you are, God has a plan for your life. He wants you to be successful, have all your needs met and live a life of victory. God wants every day of your life to be a day full of peace and joy, but it all begins with Jesus being your Lord and Savior. If you have never accepted Jesus as your Lord and Savior, please pray this prayer with me right now:

Jesus, I confess that I am a sinner. I realize I can't do this on my own. I believe with my heart and confess with my mouth that you died on the cross for my sins and sicknesses and arose from the dead. I ask you to be the Lord and Savior of my life. I thank you for forgiving me of my sins and loving me enough to give your life for me. I thank you that I am now a child of God! I now ask you for the Baptism of the Holy Spirit. You said in Your Word that it was a free gift so I receive it now. I thank you for my Heavenly prayer language!

We encourage you to become involved in a solid Bible based church. If you need help finding a church in your area, we would be more than happy to help.

Begin reading your Bible and praying in the Spirit daily. Now it is time to start developing your relationship with your Heavenly Father and growing in the Lord - and don't forget to tell someone about what Jesus did for you! Remember that God is good and He has good things in store for you!

If you prayed this prayer, would like assistance in locating a local church or this book has impacted your life, we would love to hear from you!

www.ChadGonzales.com